Gray
Wolves

written and photographed
by Lynn M. Stone

Lerner Publications Company • Minneapolis

For Brittany

Additional photographs are reproduced through the courtesy of: © William Muñoz, p.28.

Copyright © 2004 by Lynn M. Stone

Lerner Publications Company
A division of Lerner Publishing Group
241 First Avenue North
Minneapolis, MN 55401 U.S.A

Website address: www.lernerbooks.com

Library of Congress Cataloging-in-Publication Data

Stone, Lynn M.
    Gray wolves / written and photographed by Lynn M. Stone.
       p.   cm. — (Early bird nature books)
    Includes index.
    Contents: The gray wolf—Wolf country—The wolf pack—
Hunting—Raising babies—Wolves and people.
    ISBN: 0–8225–3050–3 (lib. bdg. : alk. paper)
    1. Wolves—Juvenile literature. [1. Wolves.] I. Title.
II. Series.
    QL737.C22S7625 2004
    599.773—dc21   2003010518

Manufactured in the United States of America
1 2 3 4 5 6 – JR – 09 08 07 06 05 04

Contents

The gray wolf lives in many places in the world. The striped areas show where the gray wolf lives in North America.

ALASKA (USA)

CANADA

UNITED STATES

N

Be a Word Detective

Can you find these words as you read about the gray wolf?
Be a detective and try to figure out what they mean.
You can turn to the glossary on page 46 for help.

alpha	mammals	pups
canids	muzzle	scavenging
den	pack	scent posts
endangered	predators	territory
habitats	prey	tundra

5

Chapter 1

Gray wolves are also called timber wolves. How many kinds of wolves live in North America?

The Gray Wolf

The night is quiet. Suddenly there is a long, sad howl. Another howl answers. More howls fill the darkness. Wolves are calling to one another.

Two kinds of wolves live in North America. They are the gray wolf and the red wolf. This book is about the gray wolf.

This is a red wolf. Red wolves once lived throughout the southeastern part of the United States.

These three wolves are different colors. But they are all called gray wolves. The gray wolf's scientific name is Canis lupis.

Gray wolves are mammals. Mammals are animals who feed their babies milk. All mammals have hair on their bodies.

Wolves have thick hair called fur. Thick fur helps to keep wolves warm in the winter. Some gray wolves have gray fur. But a gray wolf's fur may also be brown, white, black, silver, or tan.

The gray wolf belongs to a family of mammals called canids (KAY-nihdz). Foxes, coyotes (kye-YOH-teez), jackals, and African hunting dogs are also canids. The gray wolf is the largest canid. A gray wolf can weigh as much as a full-grown human!

The arctic fox (left) *and the coyote* (below) *are relatives of the gray wolf.*

A gray wolf has four long legs. Long legs help wolves run fast. Each of a wolf's feet has short, dull claws.

Long legs help a wolf run more easily through deep snow.

A wolf's front fangs can be longer than 2 inches. That's about as long as your finger!

Gray wolves have long, narrow noses. A wolf's nose and jaws are called its muzzle. A wolf's jaws have many sharp teeth.

Chapter 2

Gray wolves can live wherever they can find food. What do we call the places where a wolf can live?

Wolf Country

The gray wolf can live in many kinds of places. The places where the wolf can live are called habitats (HAB-uh-tats). A wolf's habitat may be a forest. Or it may be a grassy area.

Most gray wolves live in places that have both grass and evergreen trees. Evergreen trees are trees that stay green all year long.

This forest in northern Wisconsin is a good home for gray wolves.

Another kind of gray wolf habitat is tundra. Tundra is land in the far north, where the weather is cold. No big trees grow on the tundra. But tiny trees and other plants cover the ground in the summer. The plants are only a few inches tall.

The ground in the tundra stays frozen most of the year. In the summer, the ice on top of the ground melts. The water from the melted ice makes ponds and swamps.

Many gray wolves live in the Rocky Mountains of the United States and Canada. These wolves are in Montana.

Gray wolves live in most of Canada. They also live in Alaska and in some other parts of the United States.

Chapter 3

Most wolves live together in families. What is a family of wolves called?

The Wolf Pack

Most gray wolves are part of a pack. A pack is a family of wolves. It has at least two adult wolves and their babies. A pack usually has five to seven members.

Each wolf has a special place in the pack. Older, larger wolves are more important in the pack than younger or weaker wolves.

Pack members lick each other and touch noses to say hello.

The strongest male wolf in the pack is the alpha male.
The strongest female is the alpha female.

The strongest members of the pack are the leaders. These leaders are called alpha (AL-fuh) wolves. The alpha wolves decide where the pack sleeps. And they decide when the pack looks for food. Alpha wolves put their ears forward and hold their tails high. They are telling other wolves that they are important.

Wolves are usually friendly to other members of their pack. They whine and wag their tails to welcome each other. Weaker wolves crouch down or roll over when greeting stronger wolves. This is how weaker wolves show respect to stronger members of the pack.

The wolf on the ground knows the other wolf is stronger than it is.

Most wolf packs live in a home area called a territory. A territory is like a neighborhood. A wolf pack's territory can be huge. It can be the size of a large city!

A wolf pack doesn't want wolves from other places to come into its territory. The pack may fight other wolves to make them go away.

Pack members don't fight often. But sometimes they fight over scraps of food. A young wolf may fight to try to become an alpha wolf.

This wolf is marking its territory with urine.

Wolves mark the edges of their territory so other wolves will stay away. The wolves make scratch marks on trees and logs. And they make scent (SENT) posts. Scent posts are places where wolves leave urine or droppings. Scent posts tell wolves where other wolves have been. When a wolf finds another pack's territory markings, the wolf usually goes away.

The way a wolf moves its body shows how the wolf feels. This wolf is telling other wolves to stay away from its food.

Wolves also tell one another things by making sounds. Wolves make many different sounds. Wolves whimper, growl, bark, and even squeak. And they howl.

Scientists don't know for sure why wolves howl. But a wolf probably howls to let other wolves know where it is. Howling can scare other wolves out of a pack's territory. Wolves may also howl to find each other.

If a wolf can't find its pack, the wolf howls. Then the wolf listens for the howls of the other wolves in its pack. The wolf moves toward the howls to find its pack.

Chapter 4

Wolves hunt and eat other animals. What kinds of animals do wolves eat?

Hunting

Wolves are meat eaters. Wolves get most of their meat by killing other animals. Animals who hunt and kill other animals are called predators (PREH-duh-turz). The animals that predators hunt and eat are called prey (PRAY). Wolves will also eat dead animals that they find. This is called scavenging (SKAV-uhn-jing).

Sometimes wolves hunt small animals, such as birds or rabbits. But wolves usually hunt large animals, such as deer.

Wolves are fast and strong. But some prey can be dangerous to wolves. Animals may have sharp horns or antlers that could hurt a wolf. A large animal could kill a wolf by kicking it.

Wolves hunt small animals such as beavers (above) and large animals such as caribou (left). Caribou are a type of northern deer.

A wolf can smell a moose from more than 1 mile away. That's like being able to smell a hamburger from several blocks away!

It is hard for one wolf to hunt a large animal. So a pack of wolves hunts together. By working together, wolves can kill big animals.

Wolves use their eyes, ears, and noses to find prey. Wolves may see, hear, or smell prey. Wolves can smell their prey from far away.

Sometimes wolves find a prey animal that is alone. Other times, wolves find a group of prey animals. Then the wolves have to choose which animal to hunt. They usually pick the animal that will be easiest to kill. They choose the youngest, oldest, or sickest animal of the group. Young, old, or sick animals are easier to catch than fast animals.

This moose and her baby would be good prey for a pack of gray wolves.

Wolves can run fast for at least 20 minutes. But wolves often stop chasing their prey before that.

The wolves move toward the prey animal they have chosen. They try to catch it quickly so it doesn't get away. If the animal runs, the wolves chase it. Wolves can run long distances without getting tired. But they stop chasing prey if they fall too far behind.

Wolves have strong jaws and sharp teeth. When wolves catch an animal, they bite it with their teeth. They drag it down to the ground.

Wolves eat small animals in one meal. But wolves get several meals out of a large animal such as a deer.

The pack attacks the animal to kill it. The wolves begin to eat. The strongest wolves eat first. Weaker wolves have to wait.

When the wolves are done eating, they bury the animal in the ground or under the snow. They return when they are hungry again. The wolves dig up the animal and eat more of it. When all the meat is gone, the pack must hunt again.

Chapter 5

An alpha female may have as many as 11 babies at a time. What are baby wolves called?

Raising Babies

In the spring, a wolf pack's alpha female has babies. Baby wolves are called pups. A mother wolf usually has six pups at a time.

Wolf pups are born in a den. A den is a safe place. It is usually a hole in the ground. The newborn pups stay in the den with their mother. The pack brings food for the mother wolf. The pups drink their mother's milk.

Some wolves use the same den every year. But sometimes a pack digs a new den.

Newborn wolf pups are tiny, wiggly balls of fur. They weigh just 1 pound. They can't see or hear at first. The pups' eyes open when they are 12 days old. Then they start to learn to walk.

When they are three weeks old, the pups crawl out of the den. They play with each other. They roll around. They chase butterflies and grasshoppers.

Pups play and explore around the den.

Pups must learn how to greet older wolves. This pup is licking an older wolf's muzzle to greet it.

Each pup knows its mother, brothers, and sisters well. The family lived together in the den for three weeks. But the pups must get to know the other wolves in the pack.

Pack members teach the pups to show respect to older wolves. Members of the pack also help the mother watch the pups. When the pups are eight weeks old, they can eat meat. Then the adult wolves bring food for the pups.

These pups are playing with their mother. Play fighting teaches pups how to hunt.

The pups must learn to hunt. They watch how the pack catches prey. They also learn to hunt by pretending to fight with their brothers and sisters. By early autumn, the pups are ready to hunt with the pack.

Young wolves usually leave the pack before they are two years old. By then, the wolves are fully grown. They are old enough to start families of their own.

The young wolves leave their pack's territory. Each wolf lives alone until it finds a mate. The wolf and its mate look for their own territory. Then they have pups of their own. They start a new pack.

A wolf who lives and travels alone is called a lone wolf.

Chapter 6

Most adult wolves are safe from other predators. What is the main enemy of the gray wolf?

Wolves and People

Most wolves die from old age, sickness, or hunger. Sometimes young, old, or sick wolves are hunted by other predators. But the main enemies of gray wolves are people.

Long ago, gray wolves lived in many places. But then people moved into the places where wolves lived. These people built farms, homes, and cities. Wolves and their prey had fewer places to live.

Wolves and their prey need lots of space to live in.

People have made up many stories about wild wolves killing people. But gray wolves usually avoid people.

People were afraid of wolves. They were afraid that wolves would attack them or kill their farm animals. Some wolves did kill farm animals. But most wolves stayed away from people. People were still afraid. They killed many wolves.

People also killed wolves to protect game animals. Game animals are animals such as deer that people hunt for food or for sport. Wolves hunt game animals for food. Wolves usually kill only the weakest animals. But people didn't want to share the game animals with wolves.

Sometimes wolves and people hunt the same animals, such as deer. If people kill too many animals, wolves will have less food to eat.

Gray wolves once lived in most of North America. By the 1960s, they lived only in Canada, Alaska, and parts of Minnesota.

By the 1960s, the gray wolf was endangered in most of the United States. An endangered animal is an animal that is in danger of dying out forever.

Scientists began to study the gray wolf. They learned where the wolf traveled. They learned what the wolf ate. And they learned how the wolf hunted its prey. As people learned more about the gray wolf, they wanted to protect it.

Scientists put collars with tiny radios on some wolves. The radios send signals. Scientists use the signals to follow the wolves.

It is illegal to hunt wolves in much of the United States.

In 1973, the U.S. government made laws to protect the gray wolf. People were not allowed to kill wolves, except in Alaska. The wolves had babies. Soon there were more gray wolves.

People also put some wild gray wolves into Yellowstone National Park. Wolves are safe in national parks in the U.S. and Canada. People can visit the parks to see and hear wolves. Other people are just glad to know that gray wolves are no longer endangered.

The International Wolf Center in Ely, Minnesota, has 45,000 visitors each year. People visit the center to learn more about gray wolves.

On Sharing a Book

As you know, adults greatly influence a child's attitude toward reading. When a child sees you read, or when you share a book with a child, you're sending a message that reading is important. Show the child that reading a book together is important to you. Find a comfortable, quiet place. Turn off the television and limit other distractions, such as telephone calls.

Be prepared to start slowly. Take turns reading parts of this book. Stop and talk about what you're reading. Talk about the photographs. You may find that much of the shared time is spent discussing just a few pages. This discussion time is valuable for both of you, so don't move through the book too quickly. If the child begins to lose interest, stop reading. Continue sharing the book at another time. When you do pick up the book again, be sure to revisit the parts you have already read. Most importantly, enjoy the book!

Be a Vocabulary Detective

You will find a word list on page 5. Words selected for this list are important to the understanding of the topic of this book. Encourage the child to be a word detective and search for the words as you read the book together. Talk about what the words mean and how they are used in the sentence. Do any of these words have more than one meaning? You will find these words defined in a glossary on page 46.

What about Questions?

Use questions to make sure the child understands the information in this book. Here are some suggestions:

> What did this paragraph tell us? What does this picture show? What do you think we'll learn about next? What animals are related to gray wolves? Could a pack of gray wolves live in your backyard? Why/Why not? How do wolves talk to each other? What do wolves eat? Why do gray wolves hunt in packs? What are baby wolves called? When does a gray wolf leave its family? How do people cause problems for gray wolves? What do you think it's like being a gray wolf? What is your favorite part of the book? Why?

If the child has questions, don't hesitate to respond with questions of your own, such as: What do *you* think? Why? What is it that you don't know? If the child can't remember certain facts, turn to the index.

Introducing the Index

The index is an important learning tool. It helps readers get information quickly without searching throughout the whole book. Turn to the index on page 47. Choose an entry, such as *hunting*, and ask the child to use the index to find out what animals a gray wolf hunts. Repeat this exercise with as many entries as you like. Ask the child to point out the differences between an index and a glossary. (The index helps readers find information quickly, while the glossary tells readers what words mean.)

Where in the World?

Many plants and animals found in the Early Bird Nature Books series live in parts of the world other than the United States. Encourage the child to find the places mentioned in this book on a world map or globe. Take time to talk about climate, terrain, and how you might live in such places.

All the World in Metric!

Although our monetary system is in metric units (based on multiples of 10), the United States is one of the few countries in the world that does not use the metric system of measurement. Here are some conversion activities you and the child can do using a calculator:

WHEN YOU KNOW:	MULTIPLY BY:	TO FIND:
miles	1.609	kilometers
feet	0.3048	meters
inches	2.54	centimeters
gallons	3.785	liters
tons	0.907	metric tons
pounds	0.454	kilograms

Activities

Make up a story about gray wolves. Be sure to include information from this book. Draw or paint pictures to illustrate your story.

Go to the library or visit websites to learn more about gray wolves. The website run by the International Wolf Center in Ely, Minnesota (www.wolf.org), is a good place to start.

Pretend to be a gray wolf. How do you eat? What sounds do you make?

Glossary

alpha: a leader of a group of wolves

canids (KAY-nihdz): the family of animals that the gray wolf belongs to

den: a hidden, safe place

endangered: in danger of dying out

habitats: areas where a kind of animal can live and grow

mammals: animals who feed their babies milk and have hair on their bodies

muzzle: an animal's nose and jaws

pack: a group of wolves

predators (PREH-duh-turz): animals who hunt other animals

prey (PRAY): animals who are hunted and eaten by other animals

pups: baby wolves

scavenging (SKAV-uhn-jing): eating animals that were already dead

scent (SENT) posts: places where animals leave urine or droppings to mark their territories

territory: an animal's very own place. Gray wolves mark their territories so other wolves will stay away.

tundra: land in the far north, where the weather is cold

Index

Pages listed in **bold** type refer to photographs.

About the Author

Lynn M. Stone is an author and wildlife photographer who has written more than 400 books for young readers about wildlife and natural history. Mr. Stone enjoys fishing and travel and, of course, photographing wildlife. He is a former teacher and lives with his family in St. Charles, Illinois.